JUSTICE
for
GREECE

Written and Published by
THE JUSTICE FOR GREECE COMMITTEE
1308 18th Street, N.W.
Washington 6, D. C.

March, 1946

THE
JUSTICE FOR GREECE
COMMITTEE

•

JUSTICE *for* GREECE

THIS is a case for Greece. It is a case brought not by the Greeks themselves but by their American friends.

The motives of these friends are three-fold. First, there are many persons, in America and other lands, who want to see justice done, abstractly, for its own sake. To such persons the case of Greece makes an irresistible appeal. Second, many Americans are conscious of their own indebtedness to the Greeks and to the Greek spirit. What they can do in return, they feel, is a small acknowledgment of the obligation, not only to their friends, but to themselves as men of honor. Third, many Americans look forward in hopeful anticipation to a better adjustment of international affairs in which amity among nations will be promoted and in which the basis for disagreements, disputes and violence will be eradicated or minimized. They believe that the cause of justice for small nations, such as Greece, should be wholeheartedly embraced as a part of the larger aspiration for justice and peace throughout the world.

Greece is our ally. Greece has been our loyal champion and defender in the vicissitudes of war. Greece can be and will be our loyal and ardent friend in the pursuits of peace. Our aims in war and peace have been indissolubly conjoined. Just as we stood shoulder to shoulder and heart to heart with the gallant Greeks in their resistance to barbarous invasion, so we can, should and will align ourselves with these our brothers in the accomplishments of the more felicitous days that we confidently expect.

We have been prone, perhaps, to forget this true character of alliance in the relationship of the Greeks and ourselves. Greece is not a dependency. Greece is not an "international question." Greece is not a conglomerate of political polemics. Greece is not a dispute. Greece is an honored and honorable ally.

Some of this forgetfulness on the part of Greece's associates may properly be attributed to domestic difficulties that have arisen

within Greece itself. There has been within Greece some considerable degree of uneasiness. There have been not merely
sharp differences of opinion but outbreaks of violence. This
should have been, after all, hardly surprising in a country that
had been occupied for four long and bitter years by a rapacious
and implacable enemy. It would have been history's most incredible phenomenon if Greek liberation had been followed
instantaneously by a Utopian era of peace, sobriety and unshaken
brotherly love.

Nevertheless, with the internal difficulties that Greece has
encountered, we are not properly concerned, nor do we propose
to deal. We hold, in the first place, that internal differences of
ideology are not in themselves any sufficient justification for
making the Homeland of the Hellenes an international battle-
ground in a war of ideas. Even more significant, however, is the
fact that the Greeks themselves have proposed to solve these
ideological problems in precisely the fashion to which we are
committed and of which we approve, namely, by an appeal
to the will of the electorate as a whole in a fair, impartial and
sober election. That is the mode of democracy. The Greeks themselves have shown that they are willing and eager to adopt it.
They have invited us to observe, in the fullest detail, the mode
in which this principle is put into practice. More than that we
cannot ask. We respectfully suggest that differences of political
opinion within Greece are the proper concern of Greece and we
propose to advance the cause and to plead the case of the Greeks
as Greeks in the whole family of nations without regard to
party platforms, peculiar ideologies or charges or counter-charges
that may be brought up in the inevitable course of the transition
from war to peace and from occupation to freedom.

We may not forget the fact that it was the Greek people as
a unit who were our significant allies in our fight against the
Germans, the Italians and the Japanese, and all their satellites.

Our Early Ally

Greece was, indeed, one of our first allies to take the field.
The Italians undertook to profit by the German plans for an

for GREECE

advance into the Low Countries; undertook, both on their own initiative and at the behest of Hitler, the extermination of the Greek bastion of resistance in the Balkans. It is now obvious that the Italian occupation of Albania in 1939 was the prelude to this maneuver. It is obvious that the Italians at the command of their German masters believed that a campaign against Greece would be of short duration and that it would yield quick dividends in the form of an Axis fortress that would outflank the undecided or resisting nations of the Balkans north of Greece and at the same time outflank Turkey and the Dardanelles, while affording the stepping stone to Africa and the Middle East.

The valor and intrepidity of Greek resistance changed in many of its major aspects the Axis time table for the assault upon our own liberties. The Italians went to war joyfully, serenely confident that the small, unprepared and characteristically pacific Greek people could be easily over-run. Mussolini obviously expected to obtain a gift to present to his master without making any substantial payment in blood or energy.

The Italians suffered a rude awakening after a series of quick initial successes in which the Greeks were forced to retire from their frontiers. The Italian armies, ultimately numbering more than half a million men and led by Mussolini himself, were stopped in the Greek mountains by the stubborn resistance of Greek patriots. Inch by inch and foot by foot these Greeks defended their homeland. They carved out escarpments in the frozen mountain passes with their bare hands, their women folk dragged their pitiful field pieces through the mud and slush of the northwestern defiles to put them in position where they could check the invader. Then they surged forward and took the Axis-held town of Koritza. This was the first victory for the Allied arms. It was won by the Greeks.

The determining factor that turned the tide of battle, as every witness has attested, was the unbreakable morale of the Greek troops. The Italians were thrown back, every foot of Greek soil was reclaimed, the invaders retired in confusion into the fastnesses of their prepared Albanian retreats. Mussolini's saluting legions were virtually driven into the sea.

Exploding the Axis Myth

It is by no means irrelevant to recall at this point the effect that this vindication of the Greek arms had upon our own resistance to the Axis. The superstition of Fascist-Axis invincibility had been carefully inculcated. Everywhere that German tanks had moved, the Swastika had been hoisted. Several nations had already disappeared, as nations, from the face of the earth. Britain, the last redoubt of freedom, was under dire assault; the docks of London were in flames. The Low Countries had heard the rumble of Panzer divisions, the roar of the Stukas, and had felt the heel of the invader. And it was at that point that the Greek Legions in the Mountains of Epirus proved to their satisfaction and to ours that Axis invincibility was a myth.

We do ourselves disservice if we forget in these days of confusion and cross purposes the clarity with which the cause of the Greeks in those distant mountains became our cause at home.

Equally important was the fact that the stubbornness of Greek resistance and the Greek victories over the Italians forced a change in the entire German program of conquest. Mussolini was obliged to appeal frantically to Berlin for help in conquering the Greeks whom he, himself, had so ingloriously failed to over-run. The projected German campaign to the east and the assault upon Russia was necessarily delayed for many months while the Germans rushed to the assistance of the discredited and confused Italians. Instead of fighting their way across the Dniester the German tank units had to fight their way into Salonica. Instead of leaving the Italians to clean up the eastern Mediterranean, the Germans had to divert planes, troops and ships to encompass Yugoslavia, Greece and Crete.

Without in any way depreciating the extraordinary valor of the Russians and the superb resistance that they offered to the Nazi invader, it is no more than fair to point out that the precious months that Russia translated into tanks, machine guns, land mines and mobilized battalions for the defense of Stalingrad were in the last analysis purchased in Greek blood that was shed on the shore of Lake Ochrida and the slopes of Mt. Olympus.

Even after the defenders of Greece had been defeated in the field and had been forced to retire to more advantageous battle fronts, the battle of the Greeks against the Axis went on. Greek soldiers fought with distinction at El Alamein and in Tunisia. Greek airmen in new planes came back to join the assault on Festung Europa. Greek submarines drove into the German nests in the Baltic. A Greek destroyer went into action against the Japanese in the Indian Ocean. On all the seven seas of the world Greek merchantmen continued to carry the cargoes of victory. The sailors of Greece faced the dangers of the elements and the enemy. No part of the Allied mercantile marine suffered a higher proportion of losses than did the Greek.

Within Greece also the war was carried implacably to the invader. There was no calm acquiescence in Greece. There was no such thing as a Greek "Nazi" party. The Germans were hard put to it to find the paltry handful of Quislings who served their felonious purposes. Even in border Macedonia, the Nazis were obliged to call upon their Bulgarian scavengers to exterminate Greek populations in order to keep up even the paltry pretense of a "peaceful" occupation.

The Greeks, not by ones or twos, but by whole towns and villages took to the hills and caves. The temper of the resistance may be accurately adjudged by the very ferocity of the reprisals that were instituted. A thousand villages were burned to the ground, throughout all Greece dwelling places were razed, and all this simply because the Greeks in their homeland, no less than on the fields of battle, refused to admit the possibility of a craven surrender.

Yes, Greece was our ally, an ally to whom honor should be paid, an ally to whom our indebtedness should be acknowledged, not merely gratefully but also joyfully.

Our Ally in Peace

But Greece was not merely our ally in war. Greece is our ally in peace.

The ties that bind us to Greece are many, and sometimes subtle. We are indeed the end-product of a great Greco-Roman civilization. In our everyday speech there are scores of words that derive from whole concepts developed by the Greeks—such words as "Platonic," "Philippic," or for that matter the very word "democracy" itself. These are Greek words and Greek thoughts that have been incorporated into our language and into our lives. We speak of "Homeric laughter," of "Scylla and Charybdis," or a "Doric Mode." Our own city of Boston was proud to call itself the "Athens of America." Our schools advertise the fact that they conduct their classes in the "Socratic" manner.

There is no need to labor the point. Every American recognizes the basic identity of his great cultural background with that of the Greeks.

Early in the Nineteenth Century, when this cultural identity of feeling and expression had long since been recognized, the Greek revolution of 1821 struck an instant chord in American hearts. This was a fight for freedom, the sort of fight for freedom to which we are naturally and inevitably devoted. Americans have been able to understand the aspirations of the Greek national state. They are aspirations closely parallel, indeed, with our own. The very turbulence, outspokenness (and even occasional violence) in the Greek character have their obvious American counterparts. It is not simply the fact that philosophically-minded Americans recognize in the Platonic "Republic" some of the ideas that later came to be incorporated in our own concepts of government. It is rather that the simple American understands instinctively the emotions, the outlook and the pattern of action of the simple Greek. Americans understand and honor the love of freedom and the willingness of any man to pledge to the cause of freedom his "life, fortune and sacred honor."

In modern times also Greece has become a steadfast ideological ally because of Greece's own emphasis on the principle of self-determination. The Greeks have insisted that peoples have a right to live under governments of their own choosing. They have insisted that those who earnestly wish to be classified as "Greeks" have a right to be so enrolled in the family of nations.

It is not surprising, for example, that the appeal of the people of the Dodecanese should fall upon receptive ears in the United States. Americans have always insisted that those groups that wanted to be Americans had a right to be so regarded. The Greek position is so essentially identical that no right-minded American can miss the implication.

Looking to the Future

In these days, however, we are thinking inevitably of the future. The Greeks are our allies, not only because of military alignment or ideological affinity: they are also our allies because they themselves wish to stand up and be counted on our side in the building of new world structures.

In this vision of a different world, some very large strategic conceptions are involved. One of those that we necessarily recognize is stability, economic and political, in the whole Balkan area. We have complained in the past that differences and disputes have made that part of the world a breeding ground for quarrels that could spread into wider areas. There can be no such thing as a stable world that includes an unstable Balkans. We need, therefore, to adopt such measures and to support such causes as will bring to this troubled area a degree of internal adjustment that has been lacking hitherto. Manifestly, the corner stone of such an adjustment is a free, strong and stable Greece. In this respect we are the ally of the Greeks, not only in respect to the Balkans, but also in respect to the future.

The situation of Greece, however, affects not only the land areas that comprise the peninsular hinterland, but similarly the seas and littorals that lie in this part of the world. We want stability not merely on the Balkan peninsula; we want it also in the Eastern Mediterranean.

The world highways of commerce have become increasingly important to our well-being. We do not wish to see those highways occluded by predatory action on the part of any unscrupulous power or group of powers. We wish to see a transit of the world's goods, moving freely through the Dardanelles, through the Suez, through the Aegean and Ionian Seas. This cannot be assured if the nation that fronts those sea lanes is allowed to be

GREECE AND HER NEIGHBORS

the easy prey of any power that seeks to turn its strategic location to instant and exclusive advantage.

There is a further reason for the American desire to see strength and stability in Greece at this stage in international affairs. We have entered into a compact with other nations of the world under which we propose to set up machinery for the peaceful adjudication of disputes and for the bringing to bear upon all problems of world interest the composite viewpoint of many peoples from many lands. In the formation of this United Nations Organization we have inevitably suffered from the suspicion that joint operations so directed and joint decisions so arrived at will be under the domination of, and dictated by, the small conclave of the largest powers only. We obviously cannot afford in the interests of world peace to have the decisions of such a body dictated solely by the opinions and interests of less than a half dozen major powers.

It is, therefore, to our interest and to the interest of world peace that we should undertake from the outset to build up with every means at our disposal and to respect the integrity of smaller powers which may, as occasions arise, act as the spokesmen for those points of view and those interests that are not necessarily supported by a preponderance of force. If we want world peace, we need the small nations.

We have, therefore, an opportunity at this point to work with Greece as a genuine ideological ally. We have the opportunity to invite Greek opinion and judgment. We have the opportunity to avail ourselves of Greek experience in dealing at first hand with some of the problems to which the attention of the world must necessarily be brought. We will do well, accordingly, so to direct our own action and our own influence that the background from which these good counsels derive shall be that of a free, strong and independent, albeit small, European state.

Greece is the only one of the Balkan countries at present in which the full Anglo-Saxon ideals of democracy prevail. The Greeks are speaking our political language; and if we allow them to do so, they can and will speak it eloquently.

Good men these days need a friend in court. If we can find
that friend among nations whose ability to coerce decisions is
infinitely less than ours so much the better for our moral stature.
We cannot afford to be smug. We need Greece. And we can
be assured, on the abundant evidence of the past, that the gallant
Greeks will not fail us in our need.

The Rights of an Ally

As one of the victorious allies in the war, the Greeks have the
incontestable right to insist upon a correctly proportionate share
of restitution and rehabilitation. In the first instance this means
a claim upon us for support of the Greek position in the adjustment of reparations. The Greeks have a defensible reparations
claim upon three former members of the Axis. Greece was
attacked by Italy, invaded by Germany and occupied in part by
Bulgaria. The Greeks may quite properly suggest that Italy,
Germany and Bulgaria should receive a bill of damages and that
this bill should be met by them individually. It is presumed that
the claims of Greece will be examined in detail by the various
reparations bodies that are set up and that because of their
obvious validity they will not be neglected. It is in order to point
out, however, that the early resistance of Greece to the Axis, the
ruggedness and the valuable contribution of that resistance to the
strategy that ultimately resulted in the Axis defeat, should give
Greece a degree of priority against the Axis in the ultimate
adjudication. This is no more than a plea for fair play. There
is a limit, of course, to the degree to which reparations can
compensate for the damage done. The Greeks are asking for no
more than their fair share. They do ask, however, with abundant
justification, that the definition of "fairness" should take all
the factors in the case into account.

Now, in the whole field of restitution and rehabilitation, the
Greeks have also the right to call upon us for the removal of
some of the disadvantages and dangers to which they have been
subjected in the past.

If Greece suffered defeat and disaster because of our short-
sightedness, Greece can with justice call upon us to make good

in the future for errors of acquiescence or neglect in the past. The Greeks hold that they were placed in a position of excessive vulnerability because of the decisions that alien powers, not they themselves, made in respect to their frontiers. As part of the whole problem of rehabilitation, therefore, Greece is suggesting that a rectification of these frontiers is a necessary part of any peace settlement, and to such a settlement we should be a party on behalf of our ally. In this context such a claim is by no means unreasonable. It is not mere "irredentism." The Greeks are suggesting certain frontier modifications with a view not merely to a compensation for damages (which would be a good enough case in itself) but rather with a view to the prevention of the very vulnerability that invited disaster for Greece and temporary defeat for the Allied Armies, and also to guarantee that sense of security which is a prerequisite to the gradual rehabilitation of their own domestic economy.

In this connection what Greece requires most from her Allies is not just a sympathetic understanding of her motives but a championship of her cause. Greece has been three times invaded within one generation. The Greeks are apprehensive, and rightly so. When they make a border claim they are not predatory. They ask to deprive no people of the right to live in peace and security. Greece has offered repeatedly over a period of almost forty years to conduct plebiscites in any disputed territory and to abide cheerfully by the results of those plebiscites. And this procedure has been systematically refused in the past by powers whose objective was not the self-determination of peoples but the acquisition of a temporary point of military and political advantage.

At this point, therefore, the Greeks have a right to call upon us as allies to sustain their claim to the sort of frontier rectification that would have been brought about, years ago, had free plebiscites been allowed. Now those claims can be determined on their own intrinsic merit rather than be made mere counters on an inglorious bargaining table.

For this reason, the Greeks may with propriety suggest that we as allies owe it to them and to ourselves to act as active sponsors of their claims. There is no reason why the case of the

Greeks should be allowed to go by default, because we and other great powers may be pre-occupied with other matters.

The case for Greece is not an appeal to charity. The Greeks do not want us or any one else to feel sorry for them. They do not ask that we give to them, out of our superfluity, one solitary iota that they do not richly deserve. The Greeks are asking the Americans not that they be compassionate, not that they be pitying. The Greeks are asking that Americans, confident in their strength and secure in their wealth, but conscious of their obligations, give some part of their attention and their devotion to the cause of Justice for Greece.

THE QUESTION OF REHABILITATION

THE legitimate Greek claim for reparation and rehabilitation must necessarily have two aspects. Greece may first of all present a bill of particulars to defeated enemy countries and insist that some repayment should be made. In addition Greece may legitimately approach her allies for supplies of money, materials and skills to assist in her rebuilding.

The first of these claims is naturally subject to adjustment and will be determined in part by the ability of the defeated enemy to pay. It is likely, for example, that certain types of physical and financial reparations cannot be made by Italy and that for this reason a higher proportion of total reparation claims against Germany will be awarded to Greece.

But this pragmatic decision should under no circumstances be allowed to imply that Greece does not have damage claims against Italy and against Bulgaria no less valid than those that are to be paid in part by Germany.

The validity of such claims against nations that happen to lack the specific ability to make reparations in kind (for instance, Italy and Bulgaria) should give additional weightage to political and strategic considerations when the case of Greece is balanced against that of her neighbors. A frontier rectification, for example, that is to the disadvantage of Bulgaria territorially or to Italy strategically may be legitimately classed not merely as good insurance for the future but as just repayment for the past. The total war damage that has been done to Greece falls naturally into two categories. There is, first, the physical damage. Greece, as a home for some seven million persons, as a workshop in which those persons produce the necessities of life, and as a market in which those persons buy and sell those necessities, has been badly damaged. One-fourth of all the buildings in Greece have been destroyed, a very large part of Greek agricultural area has been made temporarily non-productive. Greek factories have been burned, railroads and bridges put out of operation, ships sunk. Fifteen hundred schools have been destroyed and another 3,000 made useless. This is a type of damage that is relatively easy to appraise and that even lends itself to statistical tabulation. It is, moreover, a type of damage for which a reparations claim can be easily and abundantly justified.

In addition to this visible damage, however, there is the human damage that has been done by the assault on Greece. Whole segments of population have been slaughtered. Families have been torn apart, old women have been tortured, and babies bayoneted. The entire population has been reduced, over a period of years, to not virtual but actual starvation. How shall one assess a claim for damages for injury to human beings as human beings?

This phase of the case should be examined in some detail because it serves to justify the Greek suggestion that further attention should be given by both the enemies and friends of Greece to the need for restitution. Let us examine a few of the specifications in that case. Look, for a moment, at the picture of violent and accidental death in Greece . . . and this includes starvation. The figures following are for the Athens area, where accurate computation has been possible.

The Record of Violent Deaths

In 1936, 14,053 persons died. Of that number, violent or accidental deaths . . . including starvation . . . accounted for 438. In 1937, the corresponding figures were 14,844; those by violence were 463. In 1939, the total deaths, 14,132; violent deaths

435. In 1940, the total deaths were 14,831; violent deaths 486.

Then came the Nazi assault on Greece. The figures submitted from this point on do not include military casualties. They are civil deaths in a civil population. In the year 1941, the total number of deaths was more than double the average of the preceding five-year period. It reached 29,320 in the Athens area. Of this total, deaths from violence . . . including starvation . . . were 7,052. This is a jump from approximately one-twenty-fifth of the total deaths to approximately one-fourth. In 1942, the total deaths reached the appalling total of 44,920. Of this number, almost one-half, 18,474, were deaths by violence. It is worth noting, moreover, that in the year 1942 there was an abrupt drop in this category when shipments of food from the Allies began to arrive in Greece. Thus, in the first three months of 1942 violent deaths . . . including starvation . . . exceeded three thousand in each month. In the last three months of the year they did not reach three hundred in each month.

The effect of the occupation was reflected, moreover, in the death rates from other causes. The average death rate from tuberculosis and other pulmonary diseases throughout the five-year period before the war was less than five thousand annually in the Athens area. In 1942 it exceeded 7,500 in that area. The average of deaths from malaria was multiplied by eight. The average of deaths from other causes, excluding violence and starvation, was approximately doubled.

These figures represent a small part of the cost in Greek blood of the Axis attack.

Now let us look for a moment at the effect of Axis attack and occupation on the Greek population as a whole. The growth and prosperity of the Greek state was, of course, reflected in the survival rate, that is the preponderance of births over deaths. In 1936, there were in the Athens area, for example, as we have pointed out, 14,053 deaths from all causes. Births for that year totaled 19,636. The preponderance, therefore, that is, the surplus of births over deaths, was 5,664.

In 1937, this surplus figure was 4,783. In 1938 it was 5,804. In 1939 it was 6,293. In 1940 it was 4,743.

Then came the Nazi attack. In the year 1941, the total number of births in the Athens area had dropped from the previous figure, 19,563 to 14,564. The number of deaths on the other hand had gone up from 14,830 to 29,260. In 1941, therefore, the preponderance of deaths over births was 14,691, a larger figure than the normal total number of deaths. In 1942, the births dropped even more sharply and the number of deaths continued to rise so that the surplus of deaths over births reached 33,838. This trend was not reversed until food supplies had begun to reach the Greeks by the middle of 1943.

It is not difficult to see the reason for deaths by starvation when one examines the figures on food per family in Greece. In 1939 the normal daily consumption was 36½ ounces. In 1941 this had dropped to 22 ounces. The backbone of the Greek diet is cereals. In 1939 the consumption per family in ounces per day was 18.60. In 1941 it was 5.20.

The surprising thing is not that so many Greeks died but that some even remained alive.

It is surprising and appalling, however, to discover what was the total that Greece paid in human life for the occupation. The most conservative estimates place the number of Greek civilian deaths during the occupation at not less than 800,000. On this estimate, therefore, the human loss in Greece represents one-eighth of the civilian population. If a corresponding loss had taken place in the United States, our civilian deaths in the corresponding period would have been 15,000,000.

This terrible condition in Greece, moreover, has not yet come to an end. The Greek people have been starved for so long that resistance to disease has dropped. Tuberculosis and malaria are taking a heavier toll, now, than ever before. As a result it is now officially estimated that more than one fourth of the total population is too ill and weak to work. One Greek in every four must be considered as an invalid who needs immediate medical care. This is the continuing phase of the Axis depredation.

There is no way to make a monetary assessment of this type of damage. All that can be done is to take it fully into account when plans for reparations and rehabilitation are to be made.

The Rehabilitation of Trade

One of the first problems of rehabilitation of course is the necessary rebuilding of Greece as a commercial and trading nation. Greece is an agricultural country, about the size of the State of New York, but because of its mountainous character the arable land constitutes less than one-fifth of its area. As a consequence, modern Greece has not been by any means self-sufficient in foodstuffs and, in order to survive, has been obliged to export commodities such as olive oil, tobacco, and wine and raisins to what are characteristically the luxury markets of the world. In return, Greece has been obliged to import a substantial—in some years more than 40 per cent—part of her essential foodstuffs and the raw materials for her heavy industry. In the pre-war period, for example, Greece's normal imports amounted to about three million tons. Of this total approximately one-half was made up of industrial raw materials and about one-third was made up of foodstuffs, particularly grain.

The Axis occupation did complete violence to this adjustment of Greece's productive capacity to the needs of her people. In 1941, for example, the total imports of Greece were only 6 per cent of the average pre-war level. Her total exports (with German pressure to get goods out of the country) amounted to only 8 per cent of the pre-war level. In 1942, Greece's imports were 10 per cent of their former level and her exports 6 per cent. In 1943, her imports were 12 per cent and her exports 3 per cent.

Manifestly, then, one of the first tasks of rehabilitation is the restoration of the flow of commodities into and within Greece so that the normal operations of trade may supplement Greek agricultural production, which, under any foreseeable conditions, is inadequate to sustain life for the whole of the Greek people.

Within Greece itself, that means, for one thing, the rehabilitation of the means of communication. High in that field is the problem of the Greek railroads. The losses to the Greek installations, rights of way and rolling stock, as a result of German depredations, are almost incredible. On the Greek State Railways there were, for example, before the war, twenty-nine bridges having a span of more than 130 feet. The number of such bridges destroyed was twenty-nine. There were fifty-five bridges having a span of between thirty and 130 feet. Every one of these was blown up during the war or the occupation. Out of every five of the Greek railroad workshops four were destroyed. Three out of every five station buildings were torn down. All of the hydraulic installations were knocked out, and one-fourth of all the tunnels were put out of commission. The Greek State Railways went into the war with 220 locomotives. They came out with 15. They had 362 passenger coaches before the war; at the end of the occupation they had six. The Greek State Railways in 1940 had 4,544 freight cars. In 1944 they had 63. This railroad system had 49 express cars; after the war it had one left. More than 95 per cent of the total rolling stock of the Greek State Railways was destroyed.

The Peloponnesus Railroads (meter gauge) suffered almost as great damage. All of their longer bridges were blown up. In respect to rolling stock the Peloponnesus Railroads lost more than three-fourths of their equipment.

The losses to the road transportation system were scarcely less severe. Fifty-six per cent of all of Greece's roads were destroyed as a result of the war or the occupation. Of the road bridges having more than a 20-foot span, 90 per cent were destroyed. Of those under 20-foot span, one-half were destroyed.

The vehicles that operate on those roads were also cut to pieces by the occupation. Greece had 8,700 private motor cars before the war. Sixty-five per cent of them have been lost. Greece had 5,900 trucks and commercial vehicles; 60 per cent of those are gone. Greece's domestic transportation employed 2,600 buses; four out of every five have disappeared.

Thus Greece must rebuild her transportation system almost from the beginning.

This is a field in which reparations in kind may be legitimately demanded and a field, also, in which financial assistance for rehabilitation may be properly employed.

We have already pointed out the vital need of imports to

Greek economy. This naturally resulted in a characteristically unfavorable balance of trade. A major compensatory factor was the operation of the Greek carrying trade, the merchant marine.

The Greek Merchant Marine

The Greeks have been a sea-faring people from the earliest times. They have been the outstanding maritime people of the Eastern Mediterranean. The character of the country, a peninsula and group of surrounding islands, has made this development inevitable. As a result, in modern times, the Greek merchant marine has grown to a size and importance out of all proportion to the number of population and the character of the hinterland. By the beginning of World War I, for example, the Greek merchant fleet, of approximately one million tons of shipping, was the ninth in the world in size and the sixth in proportion to population. This fleet was of vital importance, as we have pointed out, both in supplying the physical needs of the Greek people in the matter of foodstuffs and in supplying a stabilizing factor in Greek economy as a whole.

In the first World War, Greece put this merchant fleet at the disposal of the Allies and the losses were shattering. Greece lost 360 ships, with a combined tonnage of 767,353 tons. This was 64 per cent of the total Greek merchant fleet at the outbreak of the war. On Armistice Day, 1918, Greece had actually less than 300,000 tons of merchant shipping.

Replacements of this shipping in the period between the two wars were perhaps not as rapid as could have been desired because of the inability of the Greeks to make the required purchases. Nevertheless, drastic measures adopted by the government brought Greek tonnage back to its pre-war level by 1925. Thereafter, progress was somewhat more rapid. By 1931, total tonnage had reached a million and a half and by the outbreak of the second World War had gone close to two million.

It should be remembered also that included in this tonnage were not only the passenger liners, the ocean-going cargo steamers and the tramp freighters but also the several thousand sailing ships, many of them equipped with auxiliary engines, that

GREEK MERCHANT MARINE

WORLD WAR I

AT THE BEGINNING

AT THE END

WORLD WAR II

AT THE BEGINNING

AT THE END

SAILING SHIPS

AT THE BEGINNING

AT THE END

All Sunk

= 200,000 Gross Tons
= 200 Sailing Ships

carried on the coastal and inter-island trade. Some idea of the importance of this factor may be had from observing that in 1938 more than 15,000 such sailing boats put in and out of Greek ports in the coastal trade, carrying goods of more than 675,000 tons.

The normal movement of goods within Greece in the pre-war period was normally more than 3,500,000 tons annually. This was roughly the equivalent of the amount of goods brought into Greece by the merchant marine. Consequently, the rehabilitation of the marine carrying service is an indispensable part of the rebuilding of Greek post-war economy.

Ship Losses — World War II

The extent of the rehabilitation that is required can be seen from the volume of ship losses that Greece has sustained during World War II. Fortunately, for Greece and for us, some of the ocean-going freighters and some passenger liners were far from Greece at the outbreak of hostilities and were able to continue in service. Nevertheless, Greece has lost approximately 65 per cent of her total freight-carrying capacity in overseas trade. In some categories the losses have been substantially higher than that figure; in others replacements were made during the actual course of hostilities. In striking an average, however, it is by no means an exaggeration to state that more than two-thirds of the heavy tonnage of the Greek merchant marine must be restored to reach the pre-war level.

In the category of coastal and sailing ships the situation is even more critical. A large part of this category was wiped out in the course of hostilities. Virtually all that remained was destroyed by the Germans in the course of occupation. Of her sailing fleet of more than two thousand ships of an average of forty-five tons, Greece has lost all.

This is a vitally significant factor in the problem of rehabilitation because it affects, not merely the nation as a whole and not merely the large operators who may have some credit facilities, but rather the small entrepreneur and the individual ship-owner and sailor. It is this type of replacement that will affect the actual living conditions of a quarter of a million Greek families that are directly dependent on the sea.

The rehabilitation of the Greek merchant marine is a two-fold problem. It involves first of all the actual supplying of Greece in kind of some of the shipping that has been lost. It has been suggested, for example, that some of the surplus war-time shipping, Liberty and Victory ships, might be adapted to the Greek merchant marine for use as tramp steamers. This was a substantial part of Greek merchant service before the war and while its instant effect on Greek economy may not be great, it has always been recognized as a large factor in the solidarity of Greek shipping as a whole. Vessels that by virtue of their slow speed could not hope to compete on scheduled runs might prove useful for this purpose.

There will be, unquestionably, in Allied hands, a substantial surplus of tonnage in a number of categories in the post-war period, and the Greeks are correct and reasonable in suggesting that a part of this tonnage should be allocated to them upon advantageous terms. This is in effect rehabilitation in kind and some of it can and should be derived from enemy countries and some should be supplied by Greece's allies.

The other factor in marine rehabilitation is the factor of finance. Some of the Greek loans that have been and are being negotiated can be predicated upon the definite use of funds so obtained for mercantile marine rehabilitation. Their security is obvious and it is good. It will be to the advantage of Greece and to our advantage if the terms are exceptionally favorable. What this means, in a few words, is that money advanced to buy and build ships for Greece is a good investment in Greek economy, in world economy, and in peace.

Problems of Physical Rebuilding

The rehabilitation of trade, however, requires not only the restoration of means of commerce and transportation. It requires also the re-establishment of buildings and factories through

which those means operate. In that connection the question of
physical building in Greece is vital.

The total number of buildings before the war was 1,735,000.
In the course of the hostilities and occupation just about one-
fourth of these, 401,000, were destroyed. Many of these, of
course, were homes, but others were shops, stores, railroad termi-
nals, sheds and warehouses, and other commercial facilities. It is
impossible therefore to divide the question of communications
from their termini.

At this point also, rehabilitation involves both reparation in
kind (that is, the supplying of actual building materials) and
also the providing of the fiscal basis upon which such materials
can be purchased and imported.

Thus, the first problem of reparations and rehabilitation comes
down to working with a country that is shattered, prostrate, and
virtually isolated by making that country once more an active
agent in world trade and a functional economic entity both
externally and internally.

As we have pointed out, the basis for Greek economy is
essentially agricultural. Nevertheless the pressure of population
(intensified by the influx after the first World War) suggests
the importance of industry, past and present, as a means of
building up a more diversified economy and a higher standard of
living. The rehabilitation of Greek industry, with provision for
its expansion, is therefore a logical part of any program of
justice for Greece.

The metallic industries are usually adopted as the index of
heavy industrial production. These industries are not large in
Greece but they are well diversified. Before the war Greece was
a producer of iron, manganese, nickel, chromium, magnesite,
magnesium, emory, pyrites, and bauxite. There were also large
deposits of lignite in various stages of development.

The amount of damage that was done to the export trade in
these metals by the Nazi conquest and invasion was devastatingly
large. In spite of the fact that the Germans required all the
mineral resources upon which they could put their hands, the
total volume of ore exported in 1940 fell to 29 per cent of what

it was in the preceding year. In 1941 iron exports, which had been the largest in bulk, and pyrites, which had been second only to iron, were stopped almost entirely. As a result, mineral exports in 1941 reached only 6 per cent of the 1939 levels. By 1942, even the small trickle of incidental mineral production going into world markets was cut off and only a few tons of manganese and chromite were sent out of the country. The total exports were 2 per cent of the 1939 volume. What that means, in short, is that within three years, the production of minerals for export in Greece was cut to just one-fiftieth of its former level.

Obviously, there is a very large problem in the replacement of operations, re-installation of machinery, rebuilding of power units, and movement of raw materials and industrial products before the industrial plant of Greece can be put back on its feet.

Rehabilitation in Agriculture

The situation in respect to Greek agriculture is somewhat better than that in respect to industry. But in this field also there is need for an immense restoration.

Before the war, Greece had slightly more than five million acres under cultivation. During the conquest and occupation this was cut to 3,437,000 acres. Thus the area under cultivation was reduced by approximately one-third.

The more drastic living conditions, however, the continued resistance, and the destruction of some crops to prevent their falling into enemy hands resulted in a decline of production greater than the decline in the area of cultivation. In 1938, for example, Greece produced 2,730,848 metric tons of agricultural commodities. The average production for the years 1941 through 1944, inclusive, was only 1,623,291 tons. Thus the output was reduced by about one-half.

The actual damage to Greek economy was even greater than this figure would indicate. The most valuable agricultural crop for export that Greece had was, of course, tobacco. This commodity was almost entirely wiped out by the war, both because of devastation at home and because of the loss of export markets. In 1938, for example, 205,000 acres were devoted to cultivation of tobacco. During the war this was cut to 38,000 acres, a decline of 82 per cent. The volume of production declined even more sharply—from 48,000 metric tons to 5,400, a drop of 89 per cent.

Substantial losses were suffered in some other important agricultural crops. Grape and raisin production, for example, was cut by more than two-thirds in the course of the war.

Other products of the land or related to it also suffered great losses. One-fourth of all of Greece's forests were destroyed during the war.

In a country such as Greece, the livestock population is also a vital part of agricultural wealth. The necessity of killing for food, plus the depredations of the enemy, reduced the total livestock population to considerably less than one-half of its former levels. One-half of all the sheep and goats in Greece, for example, were destroyed. Four out of every five pigs were killed. Three out of every five head of cattle, three out of five horses, three out of five mules and one out of every two donkeys that Greece had before the war have been lost to her on account of the enemy.

This loss is accentuated by the fact that the course of the war interrupted the normal importation of live animals in Greece. Animal husbandry in Greece was never large enough to meet the needs of the population. The required difference was made up by importation. Before the war, for example, Greece brought in annually between 50,000 and 75,000 head of cattle (including cows and draft animals). In 1942, Greece's total imports of live cattle were thirty-four head. In the pre-war years, Greece normally brought in annually between 450,000 and 500,000 head of sheep and goats. In 1942, Greece brought in a total of 303 head.

Manifestly the movement of agricultural commodities and of livestock must be restored to compensate for an interruption of this sort. There is at this point also an enormous problem of rehabilitation.

The Problem of Finance

It is in part to meet these specific needs that the Government of Greece has already concluded successful negotiations with both Great Britain and the United States for financial assistance. Relatively little of this rehabilitation can come in reparations in kind from the enemy. The Greeks have recognized this, and are undertaking to rebuild their productive operations with the assistance of foreign capital. The obvious validity of their claims and their objectives is the reason that foreign capital must be supplied on advantageous terms.

In connection with the loans that have already been made, however, and with the application for other loans, which must necessarily be forthcoming at some time in the future, there is another immediately important problem. The drastic shortages of consumer goods and the introduction of worthless Axis money led inevitably to critical inflation that extended from the occupation period into the months following surrender. It has been necessary, therefore, to introduce foreign capital to stabilize Greek currency. This is a normal and expectable part of rehabilitation. Fundamental stabilization of currency, however, is only a part of, and a reflection of, the restoration of a stabilized economy as a whole. It is, therefore, not entirely correct to classify any loans to Greece merely as currency stabilization loans. They are rehabilitation loans and should be so regarded. They are a recognition of the claims that Greece may justifiably make on her Allies, and while their size is necessarily governed by the ability of Greece to meet those obligations over a period and thus to avoid a crushing burden of external debt, the terms upon which they are made must be conditioned by the validity of the Greek cause and by our own desire to see Greece regain her rightful place.

The amount of suffering that Greece has undergone has been cited, not to harrow one's feelings nor to serve as the basis for an instant and urgent appeal for relief or charity. It is presented rather as the rational and logical explanation of why extraordinarily careful consideration must be given to the needs of Greece. Here within the United States our physical suffering as a result of the war has been extremely low. The worst thing that we have gone through is merely some dislocation of some of our pro-

The Dodecanese Islands, southeast of Greece

ductive processes with occasional, temporary, and unimportant inconveniences. We have not been frozen and starving as a result of the war.

For that reason, it is imperative that we appreciate the dire necessity of peoples who have been obliged to undergo the ordeals from which we, fortunately, have been spared. It is necessary to understand and appreciate this to get the case of Greece into perspective. Once that perspective is reached we will have gone beyond the point at which the legitimate claims of a faithful friend can be disposed of by a procrastinating shrug.

Justice for Greece involves not only our assistance in rehabilitation; it involves also our active support of Greek claims for restitution to the Greek State of productive areas of which it has been deprived.

THE RETURN OF THE DODECANESE ISLANDS

GREECE is asking the United States that it support vigorously her claim for the restitution to Greek sovereignty of the Dodecanese Islands. We cannot in honor evade the support of this claim.

The Dodecanese is a group of small islands lying in the eastern Mediterranean, southeast of Greece not far from the coast of Asia Minor. Because of the name Dodecanese, they are also generally referred to as the "twelve islands of the Aegean," but they actually number thirteen.

The largest of these islands is Rhodes. The best known perhaps is Patmos, on which St. John the Divine wrote his Revelation. In the group also is the island of Cos which was the home of Hippocrates and therefore is in a sense a shrine of modern medicine.

In ancient times these islands were clearly and indisputably Greek. Their population is clearly and indisputably Greek to this day. They have, however, undergone numerous vicissitudes in the course of their 3,000 years of recorded history. The poet Homer mentioned Rhodians as part of the Greek force that fought against Troy. The people of the islands fought against

the Persians and took part in the Greek Peloponnesian wars.
The Rhodian Republic drove out the Macedonian garrison after
the death of Alexander the Great, and Rhodes maintained her
Greek independence from Rome even after Greece herself was
overrun. It was, indeed, not until the middle of the Second
Century A.D. that Rhodes was finally incorporated into the
Roman Empire as a subject state.

Subsequently, the Dodecanese Islands, still maintaining their
Greek identity, became a province of the Byzantine Empire and
they maintained this status until they were taken over by the
City State of Venice at the beginning of the Thirteenth Century.
A hundred years later, the Knights Hospitalers of St. John of
Jerusalem assumed control of the archipelago and ruled it until
they lost out eventually to the expanding power of Islam. Con-
stantinople fell in 1453 A.D. and Christian control of the eastern
Mediterranean was thereby brought to an end. It was not until
1522, however, that the Turks were able to drive the Knights
Hospitalers and their Greek Dodecanese defenders out of
·Rhodes, and it was not until 1537 that all of these islands came
under Turkish rule.

The regime of the Ottoman Empire in the Dodecanese was
generally benign. There was a high degree of local self-govern-
ment and the preservation of Greek institutions and the Greek
church. A small yearly tax was paid to the Turks in consideration
of their "protection" but aside from that there was no drastic
imposition of Turkish rule. The division between Greeks and
the intruding Moslems was sharply maintained.

The First Reunion With Greece

When the Greeks rose against Turkey in 1821, the inhabitants of the Dodecanese gave what assistance they could to their
brother Greeks on the mainland and subsequently freed the
entire archipelago from Turkish rule and were united with
Greece.

The Protocol of London, in 1830, fixed the frontiers of the
new Greek State and under its terms the western powers, in

consideration of other factors and exchanges, returned the Islands to Turkish sovereignty.

In the Treaty of Paris, 1856, and the Treaty of Berlin, 1878, the rights and privileges of the Dodecanese as Greeks were guaranteed as against Turkish encroachment. There was, however, a continuous opposition to Turkish rule in the Islands and there were some Turkish repressive acts.

In 1912, Italy and Turkey went to war. One of Italy's first acts was the occupation of the Dodecanese. The Italians represented themselves to be liberators of the Dodecanese people and in the early days of the occupation proclaimed their intention of liberating this Christian Greek population from Turkish sovereignty. The Dodecanese people, in turn, proclaimed their complete autonomy and immediately declared they wished to be reunited with Greece.

This wish was speedily over-ridden by the Italians and in the Treaty between Italy and Turkey (Lausanne, 1914), Italy agreed to give the Islands to Turkey once more, whenever Turkey evacuated her forces from Africa. Subsequently, on the excuse that Turkey had not consummated that evacuation, Italy remained in permanent occupation of the Dodecanese and set up military garrisons, political police and all the institutions of drastic alien rule. Subsequently, when Italy bargained for the basis on which she would join the Allies in the first World War, she demanded full sovereignty in the Dodecanese as part of the bargain.

The Dodecanese Greeks presented strong representations to the Peace Conference and to the victorious Allies for recognition of their Greek character and their reunion with Greece. They received moral support from all of the Allies except Italy, and for a time it seemed their case had been won. On July 29, 1919, Italy's foreign minister, Tittoni, signed an agreement with Greece to cede the Islands, with the exception of Rhodes, to Greece and to submit the future of Rhodes to a popular plebiscite. Within a year, however, Italy denounced this agreement and in August, 1920, obtained from Turkey in the Treaty of Sevres a renunciation of all Turkish claims over the Dodecanese in favor of Italy.

The Italians at this time indicated that the ultimate disposition of the Islands would be determined by the League of Nations, plus a popular plebiscite in the case of Rhodes. Later, however, Italy announced that this treaty also had lapsed and subsequently obtained further renunciation of Turkish claims on the Islands in the Treaty of Lausanne in 1923. This treaty contained the clause: "the future of the Islands being settled or to be settled by the parties concerned."

This settlement has never been made. Italy's power remained in the Dodecanese, harsh, brutal and oppressive, right up to the time of the Italian surrender in World War II. The future of the Islands is still a moot question and must come up again as a part of the peace settlement.

Indisputable Greek Character

There is one curious factor in the entire case of the Dodecanese. They have been in the hands of the Romans, the Byzantines, the Knights Hospitalers, the Turks, and the Italians, and yet none of these except the Italians has ever had the temerity to suggest that the Islands were anything but Greek. The basic language of the Islands has always been Greek, the schools have been Greek, the culture, customs and folk lore have been Greek; the religion since the beginning of the Christian era has been that of the Greek Orthodox Church. After three hundred years of Turkish rule there were less than ten thousand self-confessed Moslems in the entire archipelago. It is astonishing but true that we, like every other people, have always taken the Greek character of the Dodecanese completely for granted. Unless one knew by close research, he would almost automatically identify Rhodes as a "city in Greece." We have heard almost from childhood of the famous sponge fishermen of the Dodecanese. Has anyone ever thought of those sponge fishermen as Turkish or Italian? Has anyone ever thought of them as anything but Greek? In this respect we have perhaps missed some of the validity of the Dodecanese case because it is so completely obvious. If we thought about it at all, we took it for granted that a group of islands so characteristically Greek in every respect would naturally find its way into the Greek state and that any interruption in this process was entirely unintentional and possibly, at worst, neglectful.

The difficulty with that point of view is, however, that while our neglect of the Dodecanese problem may have been merely thoughtless, the Italian pre-occupation with it was entirely purposeful. The Italians undertook deliberately to modify the Greek character of the Islands. They insisted that business should be conducted in the Italian language. They closed Greek schools and killed Greek priests with the bayonet at their very altars. They undertook, in short, to make over a temporary strategic position which they had wrested from Turkey into a permanent ethnic position by the forced mutation into synthetic Italians of a people that had been Greeks for three thousand years.

Such an experiment was obviously doomed to failure from the start. The Dodecanese people are still Greeks and still want to be reunited with Greece.

Factors in Strategy

The reason why reunion was obstructed was, of course, strategic. In the first place, Turkey's interests in the Islands were obvious. They formed in effect a chain of protecting fortresses off the coast of Asia Minor. They flanked also, to a degree, the southern approach to the Dardanelles. Similarly the Knight Hospitalers took the Islands as a point to which they could retreat from the Asiatic mainland and as a point from which they could present a continuous threat to the Ottoman Empire under the ideology of the Crusades. There was a substantial degree of merit in the Turkish strategic considerations, particularly when Turkey was a European power. Renunciation of Turkish claims on the Islands was, of course, in part a submission to force majeure but it was also a recognition that as far as Turkey was concerned some of the strategic importance of the Islands had disappeared. Turkey has nothing to fear strategically from Greece and the return of the Islands to Greek sovereignty would constitute no threat to Turkey's present position.

The Italian point of view, however, is entirely different. In the Italian concept, the Islands are related, not to their mainland, but to the Mediterranean as a whole. Italian strategy of the last thirty-five years has paid much attention to the development of the concept of the Mediterranean as an Italian sea and the consequent establishment of military and naval positions that would dominate all of its essential channels. There have been innumerable examples of this from one end of the Mediterranean to the other including even the Italian adventure into Ethiopia, designed, of course, as a measure to flank one of the approaches to the Mediterranean as an "Italian lake."

In such a strategic concession the Dodecanese occupy a vital position. They flank, respectively, routes into the Mediterranean from the Black Sea and from the Red Sea. Italy's aspiration to be the dominant naval power in the Mediterranean made control of the Islands a highly strategic prize.

It is worth observing that it is this factor that has brought the Italians into a basic clash with the British. Britain is not interested primarily in the littorals of the Mediterranean, except to the degree to which they control freedom of movement on the east-west main line. The sea lane that comprises Indian Ocean-Red Sea-Suez-Mediterranean-Gibraltar-North Atlantic is one of the major life lines of the United Kingdom. Britain's strategy may be expected to be so expressed as to keep this line open and to keep dominating positions along that line from falling into hostile or potentially hostile hands.

The British and ourselves paid a very high price in World War II for the interruption of this major line when materials destined for the Far East were obliged to make the voyage through the South Atlantic and around Africa. The difference between the British position and the Italian is the difference between the desire to control a lane through an enclosed body of water and a desire to dominate the entire body itself. For that reason Great Britain is not interested in obtaining the Dodecanese but it is interested in seeing that they do not fall into hostile hands. The British for this reason have always supported in principle the return of the Dodecanese to Greece but have been obliged to deviate from that principle in order to establish a working basis with Italy.

Actually, the development of international structures for keeping the peace should modify the total concept of the strategy of the Eastern Mediterranean. With this in view, the Greeks have already indicated that there will be no objection on their part to the use of either Rhodes or Leros as a base for United Nations security operations. This is not in conflict with the previous strategic conception of a free, secure and stable Eastern Mediterranean.

The necessitous condition of coming to terms with Italy no longer exists nor is there good reason why the Security Council of the United Nations should be under necessitous obligation to make any territorial concessions to any latent imperialism, Italian or other. There is no reason to placate, mollify or appease Italian Empire builders seeking to reconstruct the concept and the fact of "Mare Nostrum." By the same token there is no reason to placate or mollify any non-Italian power, whose policy also includes the concept of an enclosed preserve in this area. For this reason, the case of the Dodecanese can, in the light of its international implications, now be decided, not on the basis of appeasement but on the basis of its intrinsic merit.

This is now the official position of the United States Government. The Council of Foreign Ministers that met in London late in 1945 discussed the question of the Dodecanese. The issue had become somewhat complicated by the Russian suggestion, unofficially put forward, that the Soviet Union might ask for either the cession of the Dodecanese or for bases in the archipelago.

After the London conference, Secretary of State James F. Byrnes, reported to the American public on October 5, 1945:

"The Council was in general agreement that the Dodecanese Islands should go to Greece, although the assent of one member (Russia—*Ed.*) was qualified pending the study of certain questions by his government."

The American position, therefore, has been established, both to foreign governments and to the people of the United States.

Considerations of Welfare

Concern for the future welfare of the Islands themselves
suggests likewise their return to Greek sovereignty. Greece is a
natural outlet for their raw materials, notably of their fisheries
and sponge beds. Moreover, the close cultural bonds of the
islands to Greece suggest that Greek rule would be benevolent,
and benevolent government is something the Dodecanese people
have not enjoyed for many years.

Some advantages would accrue also to Greece from the re-
incorporation of this Island territory. The animal husbandry
of the Islands, for example, which is larger than is required for
domestic needs would assist in the rehabilitation of Greek agricultural economy. The marketing of Island products would give
an additional stimulus to Greek trade and the addition of the
splendid people of the Dodecanese to the Greek commonwealth
would afford an additional reserve of man-power which could
be drawn upon openly in the future instead of surreptitiously
as in the past.

From the standpoint of strategy, the defensive position of
Greece would be improved also by control of these outlying
Islands. From the point of view of our own strategy and that of
the United Nations the freedom of the sea lanes of the world
would be better assured by having these Islands in the hands of
an obviously friendly power than to have them fall into the
control of a potentially unfriendly state or combination of states.

The most cogent argument for the return of the Dodecanese
to Greece, however, is not strategic or economic, it is political
and moral.

We have been committed again and again to the principle that
the peoples of this world have a right to live under governments
of their own choosing. Sometimes we call this self-determination.
Sometimes we call it the rights of minorities. Under any name
it is the recognition of the right of a body of men to determine
to what institutions they shall give their allegiance.

In the case of the Dodecanese there are not two sides to this
question. The very preservation of their language, religion and

cultural identity is more profound evidence of their genuine desires than any that could be obtained from plebiscites or political manifestos. Nevertheless, even in this latter field, the Dodecanese people have never failed to take advantage of any opportunity that was afforded to place their case before the people of the world.

Statement to the Peace Conference

Almost from the moment that the Italians landed, back in 1912, to fight the Turks, the Dodecanese gathered to approve by acclamation, and by declaration after declaration, their desire to be joined with Greece. The case has never been more clearly and concisely presented on behalf of the Dodecanese people than it was at the peace conference in 1919. A memorandum submitted by people of the Islands stated:

"We Dodecanesians are Greeks and have been Greeks since the first appearance of the Greek race in the world. We were Greeks in the time of Homer, we were Greeks when the Medes and Persians carried the war into Europe; we were Greeks in the days of Pericles. We Dodecanesians were Greek under the rule of Romans, under the Byzantine Emperors, under the Turks. As Greeks we arose and as Greeks we won our freedom at the rebirth of Greece. We were Greeks during the Balkan wars and Greeks during the European war, when we persistently and repeatedly demanded to fight by the side of the Allies.

"We declare before God and man that we would rather perish to the last man than breathe or allow our children and brothers to breathe in the Dodecanese an air in which a flag flutters which is not the flag of Greece."

That is the case for the return of the Dodecanese Islands to Greece as seen by the Dodecanese themselves.

If morality still exists in the world of affairs, that argument should carry weight. If the formality of a plebiscite is desired after that sort of a declaration, let us by all means have a plebiscite. Will there be any doubt as to its outcome? Will all alien powers renounce their claims if the Dodecanese signify once

more, and formally, their determination not to be returned to
foreign rule? Will the United Nations abide by the expressed
wish of the 150,000 people on these twelve islands? If so, there
is little likelihood of any indecision as to what will be the political future status of this archipelago.

The Senate of the United States, recognizing the verity of
self-determination and the legitimacy of the Dodecanese claim,
adopted a resolution more than a quarter of a century ago which
should still be valid as an expression of American opinion. On
May 17, 1920, Senate Resolution 324 was adopted unanimously
in the upper house of the American Congress. That resolution
said, in part:

"Resolved that it is the sense of the Senate that . . . the
twelve islands of the Aegean . . . where a strong Greek
population predominates, should be awarded by the peace
conference to Greece and be incorporated in the kingdom
of Greece."

The character of the Dodecanese Islands and the case for their
return to Greece has not been modified in the subsequent twenty-
five years. The case has, indeed, grown monumentally stronger.
The oppression of the Islands by Italy and their use by the Axis
in making war against us should have long since vitiated the last
alien claim and resolved the last doubt concerning their disposal
in any other fashion than their reunion with Greece.

The world picture has changed in some of its aspects, however,
since 1920. And so, to renew this just affirmation, the American
Senate at this writing, has before it a further resolution submitted by Senator Claude Pepper of Florida. This resolution is:

Senate Resolution 82. 79th Congress, First Session.

In the Senate of the United States, February 19, 1945.
Resolved, that it is the sense of the Senate that Northern
Epirus (including Koritza) and the twelve islands of the
Aegean Sea, known as the Dodecanese Islands, where a
strong Greek population predominates, should be awarded
by the peace conference to Greece and become incorporated
in the territory of Greece.

If there was reason for the Senate of the United States to

make its solemn commitment to justice for Greece in 1920, is there any less reason in 1946 why that commitment should not be restated and reaffirmed?

All Americans who wish to see justice for Greece—and that surely will include all Americans who know the facts of the case—will insist that our declaration of interest and intent in respect to the Dodecanese can be no less unmistakable at this time than it was twenty-five years ago when Greek claims upon us were less insistent than they should be at the present time.

THE CASE OF NORTHERN EPIRUS

THERE is a further area in which modification of existing political structures is required if justice is to be done to Greece. This is the area of Greece's northwestern frontier, the district known as Northern Epirus, a part of which overlaps into what has been Southern Albania. A rectification of this frontier to the advantage of Greece is a natural and necessary part of the rehabilitation of Greece and the post-war settlement.

Many boundary lines are artificial. The boundary line in north-western Greece is conspicuously so. What we are dealing with in this area is not a hard and fast natural frontier such as that afforded by an ocean or a great gulf or a broad river or a chain of impassable mountains. We are dealing rather with a region in which the character of the people and the character of their economy should ultimately and inevitably determine the political organization under which they live.

The geographical designation of "Southern Albania" is, of course, extremely modern. Albania has existed as a state only about a quarter of a century. The designation of "Northern Epirus" is ancient. It refers not merely to land, but also to the people who have lived in this part of the world for many, many centuries.

The word Epirus actually means "mainland" and it is, of course, a Greek word. In the ancient world this was part of the partially understood and only partially explored Greek border-land. There was an ancient people called the Illyrians who lived in the mountain fastnesses north of what was recognized as continental Greece. South of these people lived a border group called the Molossians. They insisted that they were directly descended from the ancient Greek hero, Achilles, and so they established their identity as a group related to, and logically falling within, the whole Greek area to the south. These were the people of Epirus. King Admetus was of their number. Pyrrhus, who gave us our word "pyrrhic" victory, also came from this part of the world. This, of course, was part of Greece, if one considers Greece as a culture and as an idea.

In the times of the Byzantine Empire this entire area constituted an independent principality recognizing Byzantine sovereignty.

When the Turks overthrew the Byzantine Empire they recognized this area also as Greek and actually carried out an anti-Greek campaign throughout the entire region. In general, it may be said that the people who were in classical times called the Illyrians became eventually the inhabitants of central and northern Albania and subsequently became converted to Islam. The southern group retained its characteristically Greek identity, resisted an alien religion, retained its Greek language and refused consistently to join in any cohesive union with the alien population to the north.

Character Shown in Revolution

The character and temper of these border people was shown, of course, when Greece revolted from Turkey and initiated the War of Liberation. The people of Epirus were prominent in the campaigns against the Turks, and deputies from the area participated in the Greek National Assembly in 1829.

The new kingdom of Greece that was set up after the Revolution did not extend to Epirus. Indeed, it extended to a very small part of what is now Greece. Nevertheless, the Greek character of the people in the area was repeatedly recognized and their delegates took part in the Constitutional Convention of 1843.

During the subsequent period, Greek culture was solidly maintained in the area under Turkish rule. Greek schools flourished and the area became a center of classical learning. There was, however, a considerable mingling of Greek and Moslem populations and a large number of the people who lived in those mountain valleys were actually bi-lingual. The more educated spoke Greek. Even before the Balkan War of 1912, there were more than two hundred Greek schools in this border area which is actually smaller than the State of Delaware.

In the Balkan War the Greek armies wrested the entire area from the faltering Turks and naturally expected that the part of the frontier that was essentially Greek in culture would be joined to the Greek State. At that time in the specific border area known as Northern Epirus or Southern Albania the Greeks stated that more than two-thirds of the inhabitants were Greek by culture and religion.

By then, however, both Italy and Austria had become extremely sensitive to the strategic value of the eastern shores of the Adriatic. Italy was undertaking to create a sphere of influence facing the Italian peninsula and extending as far south as possible. This area was also to serve as a buffer state between Italy and Austria-Hungary and out of that idea there arose the entire concept, previously unknown, of an independent Albania. The southern frontier of this new creation promptly became an issue, not between Greece and Turkey, from which the area had been taken, but between Greece and Italy. At the Conference of London in 1913, the Italians insisted that the boundary of the newly created Albanian state should be placed far to the southward so as to include the port of Santi-Quaranta and the entire coast opposite the undeniably Greek Island of Corfu. The London Conference was trying desperately to avoid the international frictions that led inevitably to the first World War and in consequence it adopted eventually the boundary agreed upon by the Italians and the Austrians and placed the Greek frontier at the southern instead of the northern limit of the area occupied by predominantly Greek people. Thus Northern Epirus became Southern Albania and a newly launched buffer state had a compact alien minority in its southern regions from the outset. The

The Region of Northern Epirus and the Frontier of 1913

boundary line that was fixed was set up in the Protocol of Florence, December 17, 1913.

A Revolt Against Italy

This frontier violated so outrageously the wishes of the people of the area that a spontaneous revolt broke out within a few weeks and an autonomous state of Northern Epirus was proclaimed. This was actually a struggle between local Greek leaders and the Italians, in which Greece itself did not take part. The case, however, was so plain that it was necessary to supplement the decision of the London Conference with a second Protocol, that of Corfu, May 17, 1914, guaranteeing special national and cultural safeguards to the Greek population. This protocol was presented by the great powers, including Italy and Austria-Hungary, to the Greek Government just prior to the outbreak of World War I.

As soon as the clash of hostile armies made itself felt in the northern Balkan states, the Allies (and interestingly enough including Italy) asked Greece in October 1914, to occupy the region of Northern Epirus.

Nevertheless, when Italy made the conditions for her entry into the war on the side of the Allies, she insisted upon an Albanian foothold and eventually occupied the entire Northern Epirus area.

Naturally, this boundary presented a problem to the Peace Conference and, at the beginning, it appeared to be solved equitably. The Italian Foreign Minister, Signor Tittoni, reached and signed an agreement with the Greek representative at the Conference, Premier Venizelos, in which Italy recognized the validity of the Greek claim to Northern Epirus. The Tittoni-Venizelos agreement, as we have already noted, also recognized the projected return of the Dodecanese Islands to Greece.

For one short year it seemed that there would be some degree of justice for Greece in the settlements that came out of the first World War. However, Tittoni was replaced by Count Sforza who, as the new Foreign Minister, took occasion to repudiate the agreement that had been previously reached. In 1920, Italy noti-

fied Greece that "the decisions of the Allies on the subject of
Asia Minor and the nationalistic affirmations of the Albanian
people have obliged the Italian government to modify the ends
which they propose to attain and to establish a new policy relative
to the safe-guarding of Italian interests in those regions."

Sforza's Reasons for Repudiation

This official document purports to be sensitive to the "nationalistic affirmations of the Albanian people." Count Sforza, in a
book that he published ten years later, "Makers of Modern
Europe," baldly and cynically set forth the real Italian motives
that lay behind this sudden facade of Italian concern for the
welfare of Albania. Here are Sforza's exact words:

"When I came to power in July 1920 and took cognizance
of this agreement which Tittoni had kept secret, I absolutely
failed to see how it could be of any use to Italy. Albania, to
my mind, was to come under the sphere of Italian influence
but not as a result of a juridical solution, wounding Albanian
pride and working against the very force of Italian expansion
in Albania. This being so—and bent on setting Italian policy
toward ways which seemed to me more in conformity with our
interests—I denounced the Tittoni-Venizelos agreement that
meant for us just nothing but a series of burdens with no
compensatory counterpart."

The Italian action was so manifestly high-handed that it could
not win the support of the other powers. Nevertheless, the ultimate determination of frontiers was left to the decision of an
international commission. In the meantime, Greece engaged in a
war against Turkey with a view to reclaiming the Greek minorities in Asia Minor, and the cause of Epirus went by default.
The new state of Albania, having agreed to protect minorities
within its borders, was admitted to the League of Nations in
October 1921, and Yugoslavia, seeking to come to better terms
with Italy, joined in insisting upon the re-establishment of the
frontier of 1913.

The Commission that was supposed to investigate the temper
of the people and to determine their ethnic background finally

went into Northern Epirus. The Italians opposed bitterly the actual conduct of a plebiscite and an attempt was made to determine the national character of the people on the basis of language. Most of the people were bi-lingual in any case and since the older folk characteristically used the Albanian dialect as the language of common intercourse while the younger were more inclined to speak Greek, the Italians insisted that the Commission should base its findings on interviews with older people only. Actually the Commission finally reported interviews with only fourteen persons altogether.

Eventually, the settlement became a matter of compromise with Italy and trying to keep the European peace rather than one of settling upon a logical and justifiable boundary.

Italy's Hand Shown at Corfu

It was actually during the period in which this entire problem was under discussion that Italy presented to the new League of Nations the most outrageous example of international barbarity that had come before that body up to that time. This was the reprisal for the supposed murder of an Italian general somewhere near the Greek-Albanian frontier. No satisfactory inquiry was made into the mystifying circumstances surrounding the General's death, but instead, the Italian Navy steamed into entirely undefended Corfu, bombarded its peaceful and defenseless population and occupied the island. Mussolini spurned the League of Nations but was finally forced to evacuate the island by pressure from Great Britain and the small nations in the League. Nevertheless, he did succeed in presenting to the Greeks a bill for indemnity of $2,500,000.

It was after this sort of international chicane that the Albanian frontier problem was again temporarily settled by the promulgation of a new protocol of Florence, January 27, 1925. It went back to the original frontiers and placed Northern Epirus in the nominal hands of Albania and under the actual control of Italy.

The Italians, and the Albanians doing their bidding, proceeded at once to conduct a campaign of persecution against the Greek minority in the south. Many of these Epirotes fled to the United

States. Many emigrated across the border into Greece. Property was confiscated and a systematic attempt was made to wipe out the last remnant of Greek culture. Some idea of the character of this campaign may be had from the fact that whereas this region had had more than two hundred Greek schools, prior to the war, these had been reduced to sixty by 1928, to ten by 1933 and had been wiped out altogether by 1934.

This is not a matter of hearsay. The case was passed on by the Court of International Justice in April 1935, and that Court held that the declarations in respect to the guarantee of minority rights in the area had been violated, and Albania was instructed to permit Greek schools to be reopened. It was only a short time, however, until Italy, in 1939, took over complete control of Albania in preparation for the assault upon Greece that was to be mounted in the subsequent year.

The Route of Italian Attack

The pattern of the Italian attack upon Greece demonstrated immediately why the Italians had shown such a paternal interest in Albania. It was directly through the mountain passes of the northwest frontier and over the roads that lay in the border area that Mussolini proposed to pour his Fascist legions down onto the plains of Greece. That he failed so ignominiously was no fault of the systematic Italian scheming that had prepared for a quarter of a century this springboard for an attack upon a peaceful neighbor. In the early days of the war the Greeks were obliged to retire from the frontier area, but in the northern mountains of Greece proper they stopped the Italian invasion. Then the tables were turned and the Italians were driven out, not only from Greece and not only from Northern Epirus, but from the whole of south-central Albania.

Thus Greece had once more reclaimed by force of arms the territory that was rightfully hers and had once more established the necessity for a defensible frontier area so that her north-western boundary might become a bulwark against invasion rather than an invitation to attack.

The Italian interest in Northern Epirus from a strategic point of view was not, however, merely a consideration of an accessible overland route into Greece. The location of the frontier is intimately connected with the Italian concept of the Adriatic as a naval preserve. It will be observed that the Italians have insisted upon a frontier that reaches the Adriatic south of the island of Corfu. The Italians declared in presenting the case for this allocation, that they desired to have the Strait of Corfu as open water rather than an enclosed area merely separating two parts of Greece. This sounds high-minded, but, of course, what the Italians really wanted was to confront the island with a hostile mainland so as to render the Strait useless to Greece and valuable to Italy. It should be remembered that the Strait, at its narrowest, is less than two miles wide.

The creation of this Italian position was, of course, exactly what happened in the naval operations in the Mediterranean during the war, when the Italians promptly turned the Corfu Strait into a submarine nest, made relatively inaccessible because of the position of mainland and island signal stations confronting its entrances.

Theoretically, the Adriatic is also "open water", but the entire concept of Italian strategy with its control of the Adriatic littoral and the isolation of Corfu has been designed to make the Adriatic a completely enclosed Italian zone of naval bases and operations. Italy is now preoccupied with the question of maintaining ports and potential naval stations at the head of the Adriatic. There is no suggestion that Italy has abandoned her idea of the outright control of all northern Mediterranean waters. Allowing the Strait of Corfu to continue under Italian domination by keeping the frontier at the position of 1913 would simply play into the Italian hands once more.

The thesis that a narrow strait, dividing a recognized Greek island from a mainland that is essentially, characteristically, and rightfully Greek should be maintained in perpetuum as "open water" (meaning in this case Italian water) is as preposterous as to argue that the United States should divest itself of control of Long Island Sound in the interests of freedom of international intercourse.

Are Frontiers Obsolete?

It is sometimes argued that the concurrent development of weapons of enormous power, such as the long range plane and the atom bomb, and of international machinery for the enforcement of peace such as the Security Council, have already made our strategic frontier concepts obsolete.

This is an oversimplification. Cities may be destroyed from the air, it is true, but territory still has to be occupied by men, not merely by weapons. Similarly the transit of men and materiel will be for some time to come a matter of shipping as well as of air navigation. Sea lanes must still be kept open. Moreover, if the Security Council of the United Nations is obliged to enforce its decisions, it must have areas in which to operate, bases from which to move its forces and regions in which those forces can and will establish and maintain control. The development of weapons has made strategy more complex rather than less so. It is surely short-sighted to urge that one should forsake an advantageous strategic position on the land, because one has a preponderance of force in the air.

It is obviously the part of good international strategic thinking to make Greece strong. No one supposes for a moment that the policies and aims of Greece will be in contradiction to the avowed purposes of the United Nations in the prosecution of world peace. Who will have the temerity to suggest that the peace of the world has anything to fear from Greece?

If Greece is to be made strong, if she is to be the bulwark of democracy and the bastion of freedom, to which both we and the Greeks aspire, there is every reason in strategy to modify the Greek borders in the direction of making the country more, rather than less, defensible.

The strategic modification of the Epirus frontier has a sound topographical background. The area is one of sharp defiles into the large valleys in the provinces of Argyrocastro and Koritza. The normal range of these valleys is in a generally northeast to southwest direction. As a consequence, the only major road penetrating the area is the road that goes from the coast at Santi-

Quaranta along the southern slopes of the Acroceraunian Mountains and thence to the areas of Argyrocastro and Koritza.
These two areas, in turn, drain down through mountain passes
into the Janina region of northern Greece. Obviously, the creation
of a sound political entity covering this region will correspond
to the geographical and economic entity with its drainage running
through from what will be the northern boundary of Greece
to the Adriatic at the port of Santi-Quaranta. The mountain
barrier that serves to deflect the physical and economic drainage
to the south and west lies just north of this region, roughly along
the line extending from a point between Santi-Quaranta and
Avlona in a northeasterly direction until it meets the Yugoslav
frontier at Lake Ochrida.

The fixing of a boundary somewhere along this line would
have the natural tendency to protect the valleys south of that
line as a part of Greece rather than to perpetuate the unsound
strategic situation that pertains under the boundaries of 1913.

The objection to such a rectification may be expected to come
from those who, either through misapprehension or deliberate
misrepresentation, fear some encroachment upon the "autonomous Albanians". This argument may be expected to come particularly from the Italians but possibly also from Yugoslavia.
After the demonstrations of Italy's objectives in Albania the
newly acquired role of "defender of freedom" will sit uneasily
on Italian shoulders. An autonomous Albania was from the beginning the creation of power politics designed to provide at best
a buffer state and actually providing a sphere for the extension
of Italian influence. It is quite possible that there are in Central
and Northern Albania, indigenous peoples whose identity should
be scrupulously preserved. These peoples could very properly
become the wards of the United Nations and if it were thought
desirable to preserve the political structure of an "independent"
Albania, that should afford no insurmountable difficulties, pro-
vided a sufficient degree of financial assistance were forthcoming
from the outside. Greece has resolutely objected to the mere par-
tition of Albania between herself and Yugoslavia (which many
persons believe to be a completely logical course of action) on

the ground that she does not wish to cause the disappearance of any independent state whose people really desire independence. On the other hand, this position does not vitiate the justice of the claim for the modification of the frontiers of such a state if they have been arbitrarily drafted so as to include within them a substantial population that does not belong within the creation by virtue of either historical or ethnical considerations.

The rectification of the Albanian frontier, in short, works no hardship on Albania. It does, however, propose to be an effective stop to any expansive alien policy on the Adriatic littoral. This will, of course, work a strategic hardship, deliberately, upon any power harboring such ambitions, and the Greeks and their friends, at this point, see no reason why the cherished strategy of Adriatic expansion should be a legitimate bar to such a course of action.

The case for the return of Northern Epirus to Greece at the present time is, in effect, merely a restatement of a position whose validity has been long recognized. It was recognized originally even by the Italians themselves. It was recognized by the Peace Conference at the end of the first World War when it was tacitly admitted that a retreat from that position was a compromise with Italy in the interests of European peace. It was recognized also by the United States and it is significant that the American Senate on May 17, 1920, adopted unanimously a resolution declaring:

"It is the sense of the Senate that Northern Epirus (including Koritza) . . . should be awarded by the Peace Conference to Greece and become incorporated in the Kingdom of Greece."

We have already noted that the Pepper Resolution, now before the Senate, carries a similar clause.

There is no reason for the American people to retreat from that position, correctly taken twenty-five years ago. The events of the interim period have demonstrated that the Senate of the United States and the Greek people were right and that the Italians were wrong. Italy was temporarily mollified at a high cost to Europe and to ourselves. Justice and Greek interests were sacrificed in what proved to be a futile attempt at appeasement. There is no compelling reason why this tragedy should be re-enacted.

THE CASE OF BULGARIA

G REECE has yet another strategic frontier to which the closest attention must be paid if the terms of the peace are to provide justice for Greece. This is the northern frontier, the boundary between Greece and Bulgaria.

The situation on the northern frontier is a shadow that hangs over all of Greece. This is easily understood when the history of the Balkans since 1912 is reviewed. Three times in that short span Greece has been invaded from the north. Three times the northern reaches of Greece have been overrun by Bulgaria.

But even more important than that, many times throughout thirty years Greek hopes for a peaceful settlement of Balkan issues, Greek attempts to provide measures of joint action, Greek offers of major economic concessions in the interests of peace, have been spurned, dashed aside, and wrecked on the rock of Bulgarian territorial ambitions.

The genesis of Bulgarian aspirations lies, perhaps, in a very short-lived part of the Russo-Turkish Treaty of 1878. In that Treaty there was opened up to the Bulgars the vista of a Bulgarian principality within the Turkish state that would extend far to the south, taking in large parts of what is now Macedonia and Thrace, opening Bulgaria to the Aegean, and making this, the most backward of all the Balkan countries, the largest in point of territory and strategic position.

It was recognized almost immediately that the Treaty of San Stefano had no justifiable basis and it was quickly superseded by the Treaty of Berlin. But the seeds of the "Greater Bulgaria" idea had already been planted. Since that time the whole of Bulgarian policy has been directed toward keeping alive an indefensible irridentism and toward making use of every possible border depredation at the expense of Bulgaria's neighbors.

It is not surprising, therefore, that Bulgaria in the first instance should have turned against her Balkan allies the moment her independence was won from Turkey in 1912. That was the first time that the Bulgarians overran Northern Greece and they were defeated and driven out.

Logical also was the alignment of Bulgaria with the Central Powers in the first World War. This time, at the behest of the Germans, Bulgarian troops again swept down onto the plains of Northern Greece. Once more the Bulgarians were defeated and forced to retire.

Then came the second World War and Bulgaria's alignment could have been easily predicted on the basis of her past history. Bulgaria gravitated almost automatically into the camp of the ravagers and despoilers. Bulgaria became an ally and a satellite of the Nazis. Bulgaria made of herself the springboard from which the Germans could launch their felonious attack upon Greece.

This time, however, the Bulgarians were not in the vanguard of the battle. They waited until the German Panzer divisions and bombing planes had driven the Greeks well to the south before they came in at the heels of their Nazi masters to occupy territory in Greece that had been seized on their behalf.

In the interim between the two wars, and even prior to the first World War, the Bulgarians had maintained organized border terrorism. The very word "Macedonian" became synonymous with this type of disorder. Through this policy the Bulgarians hoped to keep in constant ferment the entire question of border settlement and effectively to prevent any real rapprochement in the Balkans.

Greece had undertaken in the war against Turkey to set up a sound Balkan union that would recognize the validity of the claims of each member and make it possible to create in this part of Europe conditions of stability that would lead to joint prosperity. The Bulgarian response to this attempt was quick and to the point. Bulgaria made war on the Serbs and Greeks as soon as independence from the Turks was won. The outcome of that war was unfavorable to Bulgaria and again put the idea of a "Greater Bulgaria" back on the shelf.

In the first World War that followed shortly thereafter, the Bulgarians made themselves the cat's paw of the Central Powers in the hope once more of annexing Greek territory and obtaining a territorial outlet on the Aegean. Once more the Bulgarians were thrown back, and once more they took up the policy of border irritation.

Attempt at Understanding

After the war, Greece undertook systematically to reach a peaceful settlement of matters under dispute with Bulgaria. Greece did not accede to the Bulgarian claim that a territorial outlet to the Aegean was necessary to Bulgarian economy. Bulgaria's foreign trade had long been directed northward to the European Central Powers instead of southward to the Mediterranean. Bulgaria's ports on the Danube were relatively undeveloped and her ports on the Black Sea were hardly used. Bulgaria was not a maritime nation and actually had in 1939 only fourteen ships in her entire merchant fleet. This was in spite of the fact that she had excellent locations on the Black Sea for mercantile shipping and railways connecting two of these ports with the interior.

Nevertheless the Greeks undertook to meet every legitimate Bulgarian demand. At the Lausanne Conference in 1923 the Greeks proposed that Bulgaria enjoy a free zone at Salonica and enjoy free transit thence into Bulgaria. Greece went even further. Greece proposed that the port of Dadeagatch in Western Thrace should be completely internationalized. This would give Bulgaria an adequate commercial outlet on the Aegean if that was what Bulgaria required.

These generous offers were promptly refused by the Bulgarians. And even after a free zone was created in Salonica, for the benefit of Yugoslavia, and after the offering of a similar zone for Bulgaria, there was no recession on Bulgaria's part from her irredentist position.

In 1930 Greece called the Balkan Conference in the hope of establishing a genuine Balkan union that would guarantee the independence of each of the Balkan states. It was proposed that matters of common interest could be settled peaceably to the advantage of all. Bulgaria wrecked these Greek plans and prevented the formation of such a Balkan union.

The reasons for the Bulgarian obstructionism and the continued insistence of Bulgaria upon territorial claims that she knew could not be granted was made abundantly clear at a later date. Bulgaria was already moving away from her Balkan neighbors and into the orbit of the Nazi-Fascist Powers. Bulgaria subsequently presented to the Axis itself a bill of particulars claiming credit for the fact that Bulgaria had acted to the advantage of the Axis in opposing a peaceful rapprochement in the Balkans. Here are the words of Bulgaria's premier, Bogdan Filov, in a speech to the National Assembly on November 19, 1941:

"Bulgaria is a small nation but, even so, her action without doubt wrecked the much discussed plan of a Balkan bloc. It was because of Bulgaria's firm attitude that this bloc never materialized and thus a scheme, the object of which was the formation of hundreds of divisions to fight against the Germans, was foiled. This fact emphatically proves that Bulgaria followed this policy in order to maintain harmony among the Axis Powers. Today we stand firmly at the side of the Axis."

Such a declaration leaves nothing in doubt. The Bulgarians had pursued an organized policy whose object was the disruption of Balkan union in the hope that the Central Powers would espouse the cause of Bulgaria's depredations against her neighbors.

Claims Long Disproved

Fortunately for the ultimate peace of the world, the basis for Bulgaria's claims upon Macedonia and part of Thrace had long since been disproved. Even the Turkish census of 1906, which by no stretch of the imagination could be regarded as pro-Greek, revealed that the entire border area was preponderantly Greek in population, language, culture and religion. The Bulgarians from time to time undertook to destroy this pre-

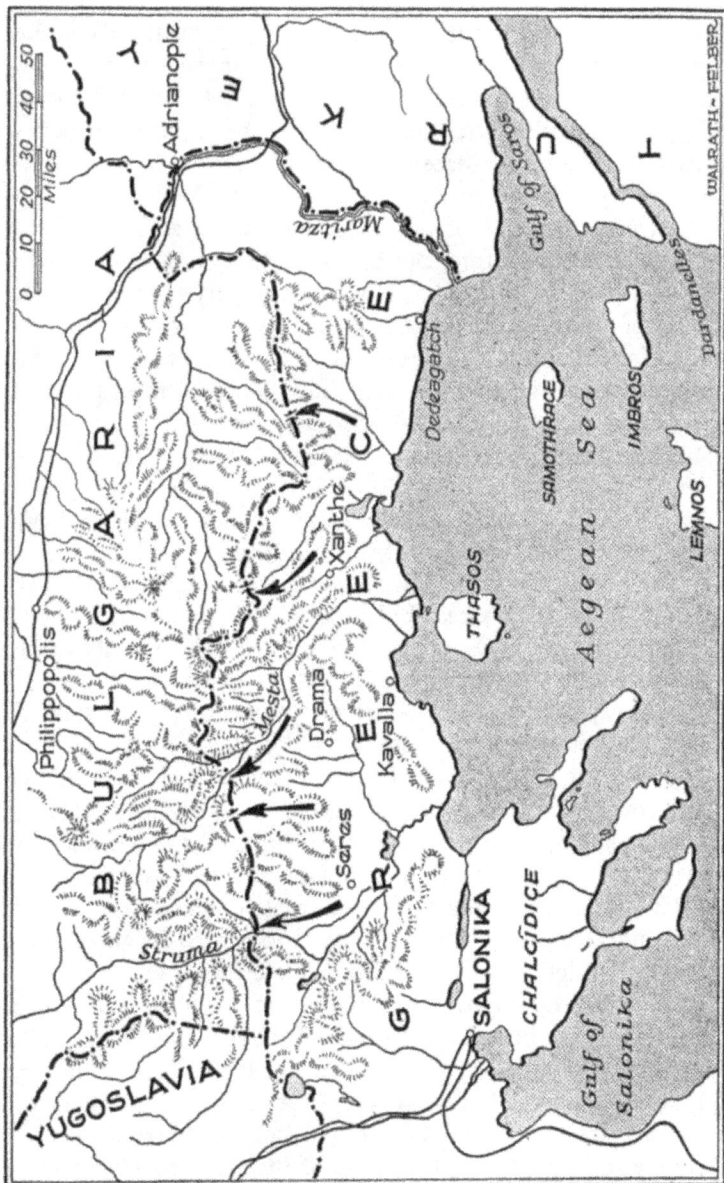

*The Greco-Bulgarian Frontier. The Arrows Mark the
Most Critical Passes into Greece.*

ponderance by systematic massacre and depopulation but the essential character of the area could not be changed. Consequently, when arrangements were made for the settlement between Greece and Turkey after the last war for the exchange of populations, the areas of Macedonia and Thrace to which the Bulgarians had laid claim were made the specific regions to which the largest allocation of returning Greeks was assigned. From that point on, therefore, Bulgaria's claims against Greece were obliged to adopt the front of economic necessity and the specious need for an Aegean outlet instead of clinging to the old standard line of the return of a Bulgarian population that was supposedly under alien domination. Actually after the resettlement program was completed only 80,000 Bulgarians remained on Greek soil and they were far from the border areas. They remained, incidentally, entirely of their own free will, knowing that their opportunities for advancement were far greater under a beneficent Greece than under a backward Bulgaria.

The present Greek suggestion that there should be some small modification of the Greco-Bulgarian frontier is not based upon ethnic grounds. There is no substantial Greek minority under Bulgarian jurisdiction for one very good reason: the Bulgarians have always undertaken a policy of systematic extermination of any such minority if its presence could be felt. Of course, when they entered Greece under German protection during the last war, they went much further than that. They undertook to exterminate not a Greek minority in Bulgaria but a Greek majority in an area that was incontestably Greek, Greece itself.

Consideration of the Bulgarian frontier, therefore, must divide into two parts. First of all, the Greeks have a right to insist that the border be so situated that the defensible mountain passes dominating the routes of invasion from north to south are in Greek and not in Bulgarian hands. The Bulgarians have shown a singular talent for placing themselves at the disposal of alien powers. Bulgaria has been the invasion route as far as the Greeks are concerned. For that reason, the Greeks suggest rightly that the battles in defense of their homeland should be fought upon territory advantageous to them and not advantageous to the invader from the north. They propose, in short, that they should not be obliged to defend the plains of Thrace and Eastern Macedonia by a stand at Mount Olympus after the northern plains have already been overrun by the invader.

Small Rectification Required

What is required is a very small rectification from the point of view of territory involved. It will deprive no Bulgarian of his ability to make a living, if he proposes to live in peace. It will add no substantial territory to the Greek domains from the point of view of area. But it will, and it must, add substantially to Greece from the point of view of security.

This is of the utmost importance to Greece not merely in its immediate strategic sense but also because of the influence of strategic security upon economic well-being. The plains of Thrace and Eastern Macedonia are the granary of Greece. The re-allocation of peoples has made them a relatively densely populated area and, indeed, without their fertility the incorporation of a million and a half Greeks into the homeland economy would have been utterly impossible. Nevertheless, these areas do produce cereals in surplus and the remainder of Greece must look to them for a part of its food supply.

After the appalling experience that the Greeks have had with systematic starvation they are surely not being oversensitive when they suggest that the frontiers of their granary must be guarded.

The second reason for taking up the cause of the Bulgarian frontier in the peace settlement is even more far-reaching. The Greeks wish to be assured that they are not entering upon another era in which Bulgaria will keep systematically alive a series of spurious claims upon Greece or wherein Bulgaria will once more put herself in the hands of an alien power to advance her own territorial ambitions.

Bulgaria's sudden repentance and opportunistic change of front after the Russian armies were at her borders is not in itself enough to reclassify the Bulgarian nation and to transfer it automatically from the category of a defeated enemy to a victorious ally. The Bulgarians have shown themselves ready enough

to change their masters from German to Russian if they could
thereby be assured of remaining on the winning side. The Greeks
do not believe that three months of being in the right camp
absolves the Bulgarians from thirty years of being in the wrong
camp. They want some concrete evidence that there has been a
Bulgarian change of heart as well as a change of front.

The Greeks do not want any power, Nazi, Fascist, or other,
to operate through a Bulgarian satellite so as to control the
access to their northern plains. The Greeks feel the Bulgarians
should be made to understand this. One way that that understanding can be brought about is through a frontier modification
that is clearly and indisputably to the military advantage of
Greece and to the military disadvantage of Bulgaria.

This case should have a significant appeal to the United
Nations when they consider the basis for permanent peace in the
Balkans. This is an issue that can be settled; and the position of
the United Nations on it can be made unmistakably clear. The
Security Council of the United Nations, their General Assembly
and the Court of International Justice should not wish to be
cluttered up for the next thirty years by a series of Bulgarian
claims against a peaceful neighbor advanced in the interests of
a supposititious economic need that has never been proved to
exist. In the interest of avoiding the basis for endless future
disputes, the United Nations will do well to recognize that
Northern Greece is Greek and that as such it is not a battle ground
for Bulgarian ambitions. This can be done by the delimitation
of a frontier that says an emphatic and permanent "No" to
Bulgarian border warfare.

THE CASE AS PRESENTED

THIS then is the case for Greece. Greece requires from her
allies conscientious consideration of her justifiable claims
both in the field of reparations and of restitution.

Greece is not seeking territorial conquest. Her national claims
are not inspired by any imperialistic expansionism. They are only
the just appeal for simple restitution and for future security.

And they are based on Greece's demonstrated willingness to cooperate with others for the peace of southeastern Europe.

With those aims in view, Greece is asking:

First, the return of the Dodecanese Islands to Greek sovereignty. This claim has already been acknowledged as just, in all respects, by the United States.

Second, the rectification of the northwest frontier, that is the boundary between Greece and Albania with the return of Northern Epirus to Greece.

If further testimony is needed as to the justice of this claim, one can do no better than to cite the Tentative Report drawn up at the Paris Peace Conference of 1919 by American experts, under the chairmanship of Professor Monroe. This report was made for the guidance of the American delegation at the Peace Conference, and it said, in part:

"The boundary of the proposed state of Albania as drawn in 1912 was highly artificial, cutting not only lines of economic and national intercourse and national affiliations, but even tribal ties, the strongest bond in a society based on kinship.

"In fact, the project of a United Albania appears impracticable . . .

"Therefore we suggest that, in Northern Albania, a compact group of Albanians might be segregated, united with their own kin in Southeastern Montenegro and western Serbia, and placed under the supervision of Yugoslavia . . .

"2. It is recommended that on the northwest the frontier of Greece be established as shown in . . . (the accompanying map.)"

Third, the strategic rectification of the frontier between Bulgaria and Greece. This is vital to the security of the Hellenic homeland and that security is now at stake.

The peaceful settlement of these frontier problems is a pressing issue. At the present time, for example, there are 200,000 refugees from the border areas spread over various parts of Greece and they are in a pitiable condition. They are afraid to return to the border areas, lest they again suffer invasion, or even a swift foray. Their production is lost to Greece.

Unless prompt and decisive action is forthcoming, how can Greece be expected to get back on her feet?

How, indeed, shall Greece embark upon her recovery, a consummation so devoutly to be wished, unless we, the friends and allies of Greece take up whole-heartedly her unimpeachable cause?

The claims that Greece makes upon her allies are in no sense unreasonable. They do no violence to us or to others. They are the legitimate claims of a victorious ally and what Greece has asked is that their legitimacy be recognized.

The Greeks may with entire propriety press upon the United States and Great Britain the need for espousing this cause. The Greek cause, as we have long since discovered, is our cause and we have every right to defend it. The assistance of the United States in this extremely critical point in Greek history can be of immeasurable value. The goods that we supply can keep Greek children from starvation; the money that we can advance can restore the normal processes of buying and selling.

But more than that, the influence that we can bring to bear at the present time can help to safeguard Greece against a repetition of the tragedies that she has suffered. We have, in effect, a virtual power of life and death over the future of the Greek state at this precise moment in history. We can through our own authority determine whether a new and more beautiful Greece shall arise from the ashes of the old. We can decide whether or not there will be in the future as there has been in the past a great and good and free Commonwealth of the Hellenes.

That authority should give us pause. We are dealing with the destiny of several millions of persons. In so doing, the destiny with which we deal is no less our own. How shall we, indeed, face the future if on our own conscience lies the specter of a Greece in chains?

It is precisely because of that future that the cause of Greece must be our cause. We cannot afford to temporize. We cannot afford to sacrifice to expediency the decisions between right and wrong.

We do not wish to be thought ungenerous. Vastly more important now than pride of position and power is the fact that we must not be unjust.

We are planning new world structures. We are hopeful of a fraternity of mankind in which the ends of freedom and goodness can be served. To attain those ends we cannot do less than to cherish the goodness and freedom of individual men wherever they are to be found. They are to be found in Greece.

We look forward to a new world, better builded than the old. Its cornerstone must be the recognition of the rights of individual peoples to achieve their aspirations, to make their worthy dreams come true. We hope to establish in our relation to those with whom we come in contact the high principles of freedom, of generosity, and of understanding.

We can, therefore, do no less than to call upon our own attributes of the mind and spirit and bring to the cause of Greece these same high purposes that we have already proclaimed.

We want from this new world four things. We want freedom; we want security; we want prosperity; we want peace. No one of those can be achieved unless it rests solidly upon the foundation of justice. We propose to live under law and we propose that law shall be not merely merciful but just.

We believe most ardently that this high hope can be realized. We believe that the very raw material of an infinitely better world is already within our hands. But that material must be molded, shaped, made into the thing that we hold good.

With these principles there can be no dispute. We have but to seek the means by which ideas can be transmuted into actions, words into deeds. In this case the means of that mutation are already in our hands.

We can with serene minds and high hearts espouse in full devotion the cause of Justice for Greece.

www.ingramcontent.com/pod-product-compliance
Lightning Source LLC
Chambersburg PA
CBHW031613040426
42452CB00006B/503